December

Damaris Zayas

BookLeaf Publishing

India | USA | UK

December © 2022 Damaris Zayas

All rights reserved.

No part of this publication may be reproduced, stored in a retrieval system, or transmitted, in any form or by any means, electronic, mechanical, photocopying, recording or otherwise, without the prior written permission of the presenters.

Damaris Zayas asserts the moral right to be identified as author of this work.

Presentation by *BookLeaf Publishing*

Web: www.bookleafpub.com

E-mail: info@bookleafpub.com

ISBN: 9789357215343

First edition 2022

The one person who taught me more than he could have ever known is my brother, Marc. This is just one way to honor your memory.

ACKNOWLEDGEMENT

My partner, Mo my number one supporter. My family and friends, you are my inspiration and truly the best people to have in my life. I would be lost without each and every one of you in my life. I love you all dearly.

PREFACE

This was a collection of poems written in December all during those dark cold nights. When I had trouble processing an emotion or a feeling, I would write it out. At some point in our lives, we all go through sleepless nights, tossing and turning and replaying memories in our heads. This is the physical manifestation of those nights.

Grief

The moments brought in by the sea
How has it been five years already?
Distant laughs
Hazy memories
It all feel surreal to me

The ocean pulls me in
Flashes of that night
It hard too heavy to fight
In due time it will pass by

I breathe and the waves spits me out
All the memories sink in
I smile at years gone by
Those days marked in the sands of time

The wave crashes again
I am taken back to a time of joy and pain
Late summer nights in the hill
Do you remember still?
The wave pulls back
I miss you, come back

Dear Little Me

Dear little me,

I am sorry for the tears of grief
That wound cut so deep.
Sorry that the world took so much
That nothing you did was good enough.

Dear little me,

I am sorry you were violated,
By those grown hands that marked you.
You cried feeling tired and isolated,
You couldn't speak something so taboo.

Dear little me,
I am sorry you hide behind,
Those big baggy clothes and sad eyes.
The memories replay in your mind,
No one seemed to hear your cries.

Dear little me,
 Clothe yourself with forgiveness,
You were too young for this experience.
Breathe in love and light,
You my dear will grow up all right.

December 13th

3

I never dared to dream
It all seemed too good for me
Whispers of I love you
They came with no guarantees

Quiet nights of self-loathing
Learning to be me
Little by little I was growing
I learning whom I wanted to be

Inch by inch I began to see the beauty
Crystal clear and deep as the sea
I stopped all the cruelty
I finally set myself free

Questions

Tell me what do you see?
A heart of gold or stone.
Tell me what do you believe?
Me or the lies within
Tell me what you see.

What do you think?
Of love or revenge
Are you full of anger or hate?
I hope is not that savage
What do you think?

What words do you speak?
Positive or negative
Do you stop and think?
Is it productive?
What word do you speak?

Anxiety

Take and take from me
Nothing is enough
I try but you beat me

A lie whispered in my mind
Nothing can stop it in time
Fighting a nameless monster
It knows me better than others

I breathe and you take a pause
I can't name the cause
This pain you bring me
It's hard to simply be

I tried to break free
Pay others to analyze me
You control everything
It's all-consuming, binding

I swim and swim
But you pull me
Deeper I go
You want to drown me

December

I was 28 years old
Your body was cold
On the floor you laid
I could hear our mother's pain
It's a memory that remains

You were 26
Looking for
A quick fix
A high to numb
A puff of control
Something to make it all okay

You were 26
You breathed your last breath
it came to get you, death.
You were taken swiftly away,
The sunset on your life that day.

Doubts

In and out they go
One by one they flow
You are not good enough
Things will always be tough

Round and round they go
Turning into a show
Nothing you do is right
Why continue to fight?

Bigger and bigger they grow
They take over and overflow
Chest is heavy and tight
I can't even breathe right
Please, I need life to go right!

Focus, 1.2.3
Breathe in for me
In and out they go
My light begins to glow

Darkness took over for a minute,
But I held on to my spirit.

December 21st

8

It's the longest night of the year.
I wish you were here my dear
Whispering I love you so
How I never want to let go

The dark sky above was so clear
I share with you my hopes and fears
Shining in that cloudless sky
Million of stars blinking brightly

The promises of tomorrow keep us warm
We know that we can weather any storm
Life is full of unexpected turns
As long as our love burns
I'll hold you close to me.
I'll hold you close to me

December 27th

9

Close your eyes
And you will miss it
All the laughter and smiles
Time will take it

Ink it on your skin
It will pass by quickly
A touch, look, take it in
It will all float swiftly

Feel it, capture it deeply
Someday you will see
It is all you loved dearly
It was all who loved you dearly

Mother's Dream

The hopes I have for you
The dreams I dream for you
The world I want you to see
All to be fully free

Take big steps,
Don't look back in regret
Love with all of your heart,
My love will never depart.
My dream for you is to see,
to live a life truly free.

Have strength and resilience,
Never let others steal it.
Be kind and intelligent,
Always remain independent.
I dream for you to be,
to live a life truly free.

For You

Tell me your deepest fears,
No need to be strong,
You fought for so long.

Show me your heart,
All its bruises and scars,
I will be here for you.

Walk with me down this road,
Let's find our way to life,
Let it all go, unload.
This is how we survive.

Left unsaid

So much I wanted to say,
it remained stuck on my tongue.
I keep hitting replay,
My mind has gone rogue

Anger in every cell.
Sadness drowns me
A storm of feelings,
I am still healing.

Thoughts

Bounce in and out
Never around
Gave yourself a title,
always feeling entitled.

Mask on and off,
Only cared when it was beneficial,
Every with you was a trade-off,
It was surface level, superficial.

Truth followed by lies,
nothing was spoken sincerely.
you took all that you could,
never giving back purely.

You bounced in and out,
and never stayed permanently.
Gave yourself a title.
I erased it entirely.

Last Call

Ring, ring, and it goes to voicemail.
Should have answered
I was too busy to care,
Before I knew it you were gone,
Should have answered.

Listening to it back,
A lump stuck in my throat,
Wish I could go back.
But it's all set in stone.

Paths

As close as sisters,
Swore we were bonded by blood.
Holding on so tight.

It became co-dependent,
Need more than a want.
Could not go a day without the other.
Little by little, it all fell apart

I became the villain
For questioning everything
The intentions
The growth

In the end, our paths diverged.
I became self-reliant.
I missed those days

But I cannot go back
That path is covered over.

Souls

Two souls walking
On different paths
Never crossing
Time ticking slowly
Till it was right

One-click
Matched
One Message
One Meet
Everything changed.

Paths crossed
Souls intertwined
I am yours
and you're mine.

When it all falls apart

When it all falls apart
Never let your heart over take you
Remember that life is not that hard
And the light will point out the truth.

Tears may be your only solace.
It's all you've known for so long.
One day they will fade away
Leaving behind memories of who you used to be

Even now it seems impossible to go on.
Just think of the road you've trotted on.
There's only so much more to go.
Don't think of the pain.
Remember the gratification that comes with it.
And at the end of the day you will learn
From the tears that overwhelmed

The truth is hard to find in the sea of darkness
But keep on walking
It will reveal itself in time
And you will see the person
That you were meant to be
Was always within

One in the Morning

The emotion is powerful,
It's the one that has no voice.
I have nothing left; no choice.

I watch from a distance
Strategizing waiting for the day,
Your love is persistent

Smiled your way back in,
I can't resist it.
Full of love and sin,
I can't escape it.

www.ingramcontent.com/pod-product-compliance
Lightning Source LLC
La Vergne TN
LVHW051250200726

843510LV00011B/1789